Top to Bottom and *l*

A collection of emoti*c*

By Thomas Lawrence

Introduction

*

Depression is a scary thing.

Of course, there are ways of dealing with it in the form of antidepressants, but soon you will crave them because you will start to believe nothing else will work.

In this modern age, there is so much focus on what is on the surface. It's all about looking great, putting on an image in a desperate attempt to be liked by strangers but this can come at a cost. Ironically by trying to be liked by other humans you can start to lose yourself.

You should know by now, asking for help is in no way a sign of weakness. Anyone who says otherwise simply does not truly care about you and how you feel, and if you are surrounded by those types of people it's no wonder it can lead to internal suffering and

depression. It's ok to admit when things are wrong and there are people out there who will help you if you dare to ask.

In this book are poems written about some of the emotions we may go through when depression emerges. They detail examples of thoughts, actions and the consequences which may result if we choose to act upon them.

I am not saying this book is going to be a cure for depression, but putting my thoughts onto paper has helped me with my own. I hope maybe this book can help someone realise that depression is not necessarily the only road you must walk.

I would like you to know there is a future which isn't dark and cold and like me, you will discover hope. Because that is one thing everyone deserves, hope.

Top to Bottom and Back Again

A Collection of Emotional Poems

1. The Scarecrow
2. My New Family
3. Inner Tattoo
4. The Dagger of Love
5. Square One
6. The Road Has Ended
7. Why Am I here?
8. Out of Favour
9. White Noise
10. No Justice
11. The Last Fuse
12. Bitter Vengeance
13. Rent Free
14. Bile
15. My So-Called Friend
16. My Perfect Night
17. Quick Hands
18. Uncomfortable Comfort
19. I'm Not Them
20. World's Collapsing
21. Sleep Messaging
22. A Different Way Home
23. Message in the Fire
24. My Mausoleum, My Lighthouse
25. New Day, New Dawn
26. Toothless Smiles
27. Broken Mirror
28. Priceless
29. Sweat, Dirt, Tears and Pride
30. The True Value
31. The Scarecrows

The Scarecrow

*

In the middle of the field on two long sticks
Was the only scarecrow for miles around, swinging
in the wind
His eyes, eyes brilliant buttons shining in the sun
stare forward on a lifeless scene
His head an old bag of flour, his neck an aged long
stick
His tattered clothes, strips of cloth for a shirt and
jeans worn threadbare, stained with dirt sweat and
the tears of the scarecrow
When the crows come to dance, they fly away when
they
see the scarecrow
The sad, lonely scarecrow
The sad, lonely scarecrow, stuck in the big field
any hopes fading as the day fades into night

*

Everyone in their life experiences sadness more than once. It could come from any situation but the result always ends up the same. Sadness is the first step in the road to depression, the first decisive step. The more devastating the situation, the longer that road is and the longer you will travel down. Many times, the journey is a short one and the sadness will just be a memory, but there is a chance that one day something will happen which will force you onto that long road with no way off in sight.

My New Family

*

Why should there be any point

Of swinging from a tree

Why should you think of death?

When you should embrace your family

If there's anything you want or need

Your new family will provide

Hate from love, want from need

They will help you to divide

Every time you shed a tear

Enough so you could drown

Your family will laugh at you

Perform for them like a clown

There is no point in running away

Your family is always there

They take you from the highest hopes

And plunge you into despair

This family has run through all of time

Its roots are hard to trace

You can try denying all you like

You are always in their embrace

Almost every moment of every day

You will never be alone

A dark shadow on a summer day

Like a huge forbidding drone

From manors, palaces and comfort

To sleeping on rain filled streets

Your used to being in the light

But darkness is now who greets

Your trapped by vicious ocean storms

Lost in forests which cover the world

The long straight road your family picked out

Instead is cruelly curled

They make you walk all by yourself

Stranger's kind words are ineffective

Your picked apart by vultures

By this so called expert detective

For all your promises and humanity

You still become a beast

And when did all this start?

Your latest family feast

Forget your parents, siblings, cousins and all

You've left that family tree

You joined the family of sadness

Guess what? Your no longer free.

Sometimes anguish is very clear to see on someone's face, the feeling they get when something has been ripped from their lives and it's as painful as if their very heart was torn from their chest. However, it can also be invisible, something which is only revealed when there is no one around to see, to judge and to form an opinion. Anguish can bring the bravest souls to tears and the bitterest minds crashing back down to earth.

Inner Tattoos

*

The tattoos tell a story

The art and designs are wordless words

Ones which are words remain

Flying dove on the shoulder

The dolphin on the ankle in flow

Snake on the spine strikes

Names of people on arms

The poems you quote on your stomachs

Reminders you scrawl on hands

Teardrops on gang member's faces

The emblems of the great biker clubs

The flowers are disguising scars

The outside tattoos are choices

It's a choice which everyone has made

Except for tattoos we hide

What of scars on hearts?

The parts of your mind covered over?

Memories you just cannot lose?

Demons you must hide

Angels have no choice to hide away

Lines which are best unsaid

What of people you love?

The smile which lights up your eyes?

Faces which scars your soul?

Dreams which shatter around you

Plans which have gone up in smoke

Mistakes which you see today

Scars which nothing can cure

Those bruises which remain with you forever

Why can't these be changed?

Time's not such a healer

These tattoos are now stuck with us

There's nothing we can do

Fake tears cannot go away

The dove has been refused to fly

Fangs of snakes sink in

Quotations and names are letters
Club emblems are just fake royal seals
Scars on your poor heart

Don't judge a person outside
These tattoos are just ink and designs
Cannot see tattoos of mind

This is all that's left
Only a handful of memories and trinkets
Scars and marks will remain

Physical, emotional, seen or unseen, pain is the very bane of living itself. Pain is the very essence of suffering; it is the easiest thing to inflict but the hardest memory to fade. The pain of losing someone you love will never fully go away and for those who suffer a seemingly endless cycle of depression, pain is something you feel every moment of every day.

The Dagger of Love

*

The dagger, weapon of subtlety

Easy to hide, easy to use

The choice of weapon for traitors and users

Some are steel, some are iron

Both beautiful in design, crude in nature

The dagger is quick, the dagger is clean

The dagger is a weapon for assassins

Expertly planned or a weapon for self defence

The dagger can kill, wound and maim

The dagger of love leaves scars

The beautiful deadly dagger of love

Used over and over, never stopping never clean

It kills with a smile on its face

Whispers sweet nothings and small lies

Without a sound, no fuss no mess

No death

Your heart is breaking, your soul torn apart

Your mind in fragments, your eyes bleed tears

Your memory goes backwards, your tongue starts pleading

Still the dagger strikes

The dagger stays with you

The assassin walks away, you hear the heavy footsteps

The job is done, you're the one suffering

You've been torn to bloody scraps

What's left of you is not yourself

A tear stained wreck with no more pride

You've taken the risk, but you've gambled everything

Paying the price of the dagger of love

Now suffer the pain but never get used to it

It will keep you awake in the witching hour

It will cloud your mind, disrupt your flow

But you knew the risks, you took the plunge

The pain in your chest, the cruel mocking laughter

As your eyes close your mind starts going

You picture in your head

A hundred thousand futures

Every angle, every scene, every word, every action

You question everything

Why did this happen, what have I done wrong

Can I salvage, can I save?

But in the end, there's one question

When will it stop?

It will never stop, it's what you have now

The dagger of love.

*

Depression is the most treated condition today. There is no definite cure which can wipe it out and sometimes it can only go away to hit back harder when you least expect it. You feel as bad as you think you feel, worse than useless with no way to escape it. The worst part of depression is that you believe every time you try and get out, something can happen to drag you back in.

Square One

*

You always go back to square one
Whenever you end on a rise
Suddenly, your knocked off your feet
And dragged back despite all your cries

You can kick and scream and argue
Complain until your throat's sore
You can only stare as people move on
The number of people always grows more

Remember that job which you wanted?
That girl you can't give up on?
Guess what? They're gone, not going to happen!
Welcome back to your spot on square one!

You may as well get comfy
Try and think in another way
Everyone needs to know a loser
Today happens to be your day

Let's be honest nobody cares
Apart from yourself of course
Even the people pushing you back

Why the hell should they show remorse?

They don't know how you feel
But they love saying what you did wrong
They point out their own perfect lives
On that they can talk all night long

People say never give up
You can always move on from square one
You are the self-taught expert
Don't listen to their words, not one

Hey, why should you even worry?
There is consistency despite all your pain
Why try so hard to get off
When your dragged back again and again?

Keep crying, your pillows soak up your tears
Keep playing the move over in your head
The wall is a good punching bag
It's something to do until your dead

Fear. When something is out of your hands, when you cannot predict what will happen or you can only see bad things happening, fear is at its strongest. I'm not talking about a fear of ghosts, spiders or the dark, it's a fear which stops you dead in your tracks. A fear which blocks your life, you can't take another step.

The Road has Ended

*

A hundred million stop signs

Crisscrossed with double yellow lines

I've heard about this so many times

But when I got here I didn't expect to find

No road, no way out

No turning left, no turning right

A sudden end to this fight

What's going on, where the hell is the light?

This road was so good, it looked so bright

But now I'm falling from a great height

I might, I don't know which way to go

My road has ended, what do I do now?

I know I must move on but how?

I'm scared, I'm being chased by someone

I need help, but no one's helping me, not one

Can't you see? I'm petrified!

I'm still alive, but I feel like I've already died

You said there's no hope, you haven't even tried

Look at me through that fake smile, you call yourself kind

This thing that's chasing me it's already in my mind

I can't escape, please let me out
You want me to scream and shout?
Fine, I'll scream and shout!
Is that what you want? I give up, you win
Now open the road, please let me in
There's fire in my head creeping up the walls
I'm screaming for help but they're ignoring my calls
Those big signs and blocks are my firewalls
the halls in my heart are filling with fear
I know I need to try and step up a gear
My voice is a panic attack that everyone can hear
My whole body wants to run like a hunted deer
But I'm stuck here, my knees in the dirt
Clawing at my head make my sanity hurt
It's under pressure, a ceaseless constant attack
I get punched in the stomach and stabbed in the back
But I can't move on, I'm stuck, there's nothing
Give me a light, a helping hand, please something!
It's too late, my mind and soul have been bending
Thank you so much for the help you haven't been sending
Sanity's broken, no way it can now be mended
Fear has won, I'm caught, my road has now ended.

It's easy to fall temporarily in confusion. You could be confused about rules, a film plot, or why are you being targeted for everything bad going on in your life. This is an inevitable stage of depression; you can't work out why you're going through it or why it's affecting you so much, and more importantly, why you cannot conquer it so easily as you thought.

Why Am I Here?

*

I can't think at all

What's the answer to my question?

Can anyone explain to me

Without causing tension?

I don't have a clue

My mind's been wiped clean

Why am I here?

What does this all mean?

I thought I had something good

I thought I was on top

I was the best in the world

Why did it all stop?

I'm nowhere and nothing now

Face down in the gutter

I wanted the best out of life

Did you hear me in any way stutter?

I'm lost, I'm confused

I thought I had it all

The one who pushed me over

What did I do to them to make me fall?

Why am I here, why now, why me?
Why am I confused and lost?
Up is down, east is west, black is white
To get out of this mist, what will it all cost?

Someone has taken my eyes
And pushed me into a maze
They turned me around a thousand times
Sending my mind in a daze

I can't get out of this labyrinth
Lost forever in this confusion
Why are people looking at me?
Are they part of this collusion?

Wandering blind for the rest of my days
Not knowing if it's day or night
This is happening right now
This is the reason why I write

I write this as a warning
Do not try to follow my path
Walk your own way onwards
Or suffer the same aftermath.

All this negativity must have a turning point, and it takes a turn for the worse. You have finished crying but now you start to feel bitter. The road you started with sadness has taken a twisted turn which is the mere tip of the iceberg.

Out of Favour

*

It was only a matter of time

It shouldn't have happened so soon

Honeymoon period is over, back to reality

It turns out my luck doesn't last forever

I'm not the golden boy any more

I'm now out of favour.

Hardly a second glance now these days

It's all about the new guy, the new trend, the latest fad

Sitting by myself in the dark corner

As crowds gather opposite

They don't even look over at me

I am out of favour

When it started, it was fantastic

I had the eye of everyone in the room

A funny story here, some harmless flirting there

I was easily in my prime

That's all gone now

I am out of favour

I used to be easy to notice
Now I'm getting bumped around
No one bothers to help me out now
I feel like I'm invisible, a man without a face
A drab, grey figure wishing for the glory days
I am out of favour

The new person acting so smug
It's hard to see him in the eye
Taking my place in the spotlight
Kicking me off my high perch
He knows what he has done to me
I am out of favour

It's very hard not to be bitter
I still do my job day in and day out
I wish I had more attention from people
He talked to a woman I liked today
We were supposed to date but now she's with him
I am out of favour

My boss came over to speak with me
He says I'm not making more of an impact
I point out I'm getting no help
Boss says it happens to everyone
It just happens to be my turn
I am out of favour

Another new guy has started today
It's easy to guess what has happened
My nemesis is now in my shoes
He is getting ignored now
He came over just now and said hello
We are both out of favour.

The moment when those closest to you start to notice a sharp change in your personality, is the moment your patience starts to wear thin. Everything starts to grate on your nerves, you cannot catch a break from anything. Another emotion has taken over and is starting to corrupt you, annoyance.

White Noise

*

This white noise screaming in my ears

It gets so bad it brings me close to tears

A constant whining sound going back for many years

I've had it for so long it's no longer a fear

Got me lashing out pushing people away

See the snarl on my face, hasn't been a good day

It's been a nightmare, my mind on full lock

Smash the face of that God-damn ticking clock

Can stop time, but it doesn't seem to effect

I'm abandoning my crew, going straight to defect

I detect I'm upsetting both girls and boys

But I don't care, I want rid of this white noise

I'd kill to get rid of because it's killing me

Give me a name and a weapon and I'll make you see

Everything today is grinding me down

Cracking noise in my head like a demented clown

People keep asking me what the hell's wrong

No answer, it's gone on for so long

So long everyone you better stay away

Don't cross me you won't live to see the day

Ending up with someone's blood on my hands

Believe me it wasn't in any of my plans

My teeth grinding hard nails digging into my palms

Gone straight into the storm avoiding the calm

Taking a crowbar to the nearest mirror house

Smash every plane of glass

Smashing very fast

Drowning out the white noise with every single crash

Shout as hard as I can at every single stranger

See the look on my face and start to feel the danger

Every emotion screaming out like a fully charged pager

Everything you do starts to tick me off

Choke you so hard your last word is a cough

Coughing blood, why the hell did you start

I'm so frustrated I could tear you apart

Smash everything, heal this empty feeling

When I'm done with you your whole family's grieving

Nothing I can do to stop this frustration

Short of killing everyone who stuck me with this damnation

Take a pistol put it next to my brain

Only way to drown out this white noise pain

Put a bullet in my ear before I put one in yours

Push you off a building watch you crash through the floors

This annoyance is a screech like a dentist's drill
Chopping both my feet off make me climb up a hill
That's how hard it is to get back to normal
I'm sorry I can't do more to be formal
I know what the outcome will be
This white noise will end up killing me

A powerful emotion, building up from so much negativity. Anger can be directed at anything; it can build up over time or explode in an instant. So much of the world's problems are caused by anger, and if there is anger in the world there will always be suffering. Not only just for you, but for everyone who loves and cares for you.

No Justice

*

Encountering justice on the streets

Make sure you familiarise yourself with it

It's rare and fades away

Your stuck with some job

Or end up with none at all

This isn't what you wanted

You hear an old bully

Who wasted not one bit of effort

He gets his dream job

People in charge are corrupt

The workers they take the full blame

Your expected to fix everything

Your love is out again

She's still dating that horrible man

Apparently, you're a good friend

Your stuff has been stolen

You go to the police for help

Your told stop wasting time

You bump into the thief
You forcibly get all your stuff back
You're in a cell now

You overhear bankers drinking loudly
They claim a record setting bail out
They then kick a beggar

A teenager breaks your window
The police then release him at once
He's the assistant commissioner's son

You go to the gym
Bullied off the weights again and again
Those guys only take selfies

There's a promotion at work
Given to someone working half as hard
He earns twice as much

The hard-working people suffer
The ruling rich billionaires are all laughing
You're stuck in meaningless living

The secret to life: money
You can be rich, arrogant and selfish
You can afford almost anything

The world is not perfect
Life's good to those who don't deserve
Sadly, there is no justice

Rage is the strongest storm; it is something you cannot hide. Every action you take is infused with the raw power of rage. Everyone fears your rage, you are not scared of saying what is really on your mind and you don't care about any consequences. You are no longer a human, you have become a monster.

The Last Fuse

*

My mind has finally snapped

The red mist covers my eyes

I've got the smell of blood in my nostrils

My ungovernable rage arrives

Stay out of my way, I beg you

My rage isn't aimed at you

But don't try and talk me around

I'll just punch my way straight through you

I've had enough of staying calm

Smiling while I'm dying inside

I'm fed up of holding my tongue

I'm tired of swallowing my pride

You want to know what I think?

I don't care about you at all

I wlsh I could hurt you in some way

Wish I could push and watch you fall

Of course, I have a God-damn problem!

You live in your own little world

You only care about other people

When the spirals of your life are unfurled

I'm raging because I've been quiet
Stayed in the corner for so many years
Now it's my turn to take centre stage
Screaming so hard the blood will pour from your ears

Have you been blind to all of this?
Does it not scare you, what am I saying?
Too many years this has been inside
This moment, I've been heavily praying!

I swear to God I will hit you right now
It's only my shouting which keeps you alive
Taking a breath increases your lifespan
It'll be longer when the police arrive

You have been getting away from this too long
Something has got to be done about this
Your very lucky I'm only using my words
I wish I were using my fists!

What's that, you're scared suddenly?
Your attitude failing you now?
You're wondering why I'm standing up?

It's been so long you think 'How?'

You're not number one any more
I've finally taken a stand
Now you shut the f*** up
Or I'll hit you with the back of my hand

Wrath is an emotion which takes control over your whole body. Your fists have a mind of their own, driven by anger and hate. The emotion which can get you into the most trouble, even if your wrath was in some way justified. With wrath, you've let go of any last shreds of your humanity, and no matter what you may feel, in the long term is isn't worth a single second of it.

Bitter Vengeance
*

The time for talking is over
I've said all I've needed to say
Some people are just beyond talking to
The red mist has only gotten thicker
My nails are digging into my palms
My muscles are as tense as a bowstring

The cold night air sharpens my senses
The street lamps are lighting my way
My breathing is both slow and heavy
I can't talk for spitting and snarling
I'm biting the insides of my mouth
But my soul is screaming for vengeance

I don't need knives, guns or hammers
My fists and my feet work as well
The heavy boots I'm wearing echo
The streets are both quiet and empty
They sense what is going to happen
They are wise to stay out of my way

Turning corners and stamping down roads
Each step only makes me more fierce
I wonder if anyone is watching
I don't care if I ever get found out
He deserves everything he gets
Turning a corner, I bump into him

No words are needed right now
He knew this moment was coming
That smug look on his face has vanished
He takes a nervous step back
As he sees the anger on my face
And the form of my fist fast approaching

I cannot stop once I have started
My body has gone into auto
Hitting him everywhere I could reach
This guy deserves everything I have
There's already blood on my hands
There is no way out for this guy

It's the best feeling in the world
Knowing that I'm getting revenge
This guy has fallen to the floor
His face not as pretty as earlier
My hands are both bleeding and hurting
I slam my boot in his chest

I'm back at my home right now
Washing the blood off my hands
My breathing is easy to cope with
The sirens and lights are outside
I know what my future holds now
I don't care, I have bitter vengeance.

You have gone completely to the other side of the world to experience hate. It eats away at you, it makes decisions for you and on occasion it is completely selfish. There is so much hate going on in your mind you can see nothing else. Look at what this depression has done to you, no one can recognise who you are anymore, all because you have given into the hate.

Rent Free

*

Obsessing over someone you hate
They live in your head rent free
You're the one who loses

Nothing else you focus on
They move furniture round in your mind
They decide to settle in

Joined by others you hate
They have a huge and noisy party
No way of evicting them

You cannot sleep or relax
Close your eyes it still doesn't work
They paint their personality onto your walls

Obsessions they lead to insanity
You want them out of your head
It depends on how drastic

You obsess on them constantly
They don't care about it at all
They are living rent free

Their good luck is bad
You wish only evil things on them
You wish they would die

Stresses you to your core
You cannot see their beauty at all
Your eyes filled with hate

You think they'll take everything
Your woman and shirts from your back
They've already taken your head

You may have told them
They may have decided to discuss it
But they laugh at you

They know what they're doing
They go further than they have before
There's nothing you can do

This disgust is the result of this road you are on. You may be disgusted with yourself, but often you are disgusted with everyone around you. They should know how you feel and what they can do to help you, but the fact they stay away from you and remain in silence is enough to make you feel disgusted with the idea that no one wants to help you. This encourages you to do more of what you want, after all you think you earn it.

Bile

*

A topic that's rarely discussed

That's the problem these days, it's full of disgust

On people's faces when they walk past those beggars

Too busy thinking about their own money and ledgers

Why should they care, those who think they're our betters?

Full of disgust because they know their Latin letters?

They're not better than us

That's the topic which we should discuss

Looking down, turning their noses at us

Driving their sports cars while we take the bus

Full of puss, makes you so angry you fill with bile

Smiling sweetly at you but you make them vile

You want them to help you, they stick your name in a file

They forget you, busy thinking of themselves

They hold you hostage, throw you in the cells

Because you disgust them

You think you can trust them

But you're not one of them

Suddenly you get the bile

Think they are so smart, think that your bone idle

It's disgusting the way they treat other people

Treat you like animals, say you think the same way sheep will

But you're not sheep, you're a human just like they

Time to make them here what you've got to say

This society's disgusting

It's rotten to the core

All about image, always wanting more

Any selfless person is just pushed aside

Always the bridesmaid but never the bride

In the end, you just give in, you don't care anymore

Only way to live is to be rotten to the core

Forget self-esteem, build up your image

If you can stomach the bile you can reach the finish

If you hate yourself, you can hate all around you

Your friends start to argue, tell them you're through

You're that full of self-loathing you don't even care

They are much better off, I've said it so there

So many fake people, you'll fit right in

Another soulless person in this world of sin

Stepping on a hundred people to gain a mile

That's what happens when your full of bile.

*

It is only natural to feel envy, you have a pang of jealousy when you hear about someone famous, you wish you could afford to buy the better version of your car. But when it hits you while you're on this road, you wish you could have everything. You become so selfish you start to imagine any number of underhand tactics to get what you want. You cannot see what you already have, you can only see what you selfishly want.

My So-Called Friend

*

I'm blessed with a best friend
He's a brother to me
It doesn't stop the fact
I'm full of jealousy

His life is quite perfect
Since we were both at school
He was already in the spot light
While I acted the fool

Back to present day now
To a difficult hurl
He has a car, a house, a job
The love of a beautiful girl

It happens to be my love
It always burns like fire
I see them two in public
It builds my envy higher

He somehow stole my life
The life I always wanted
Even his whole physique

Always leaves me taunted

He's the best guy that I know
He thinks this envy's cute
He doesn't know I'll rip his skin off
And wear it like a suit

His girlfriend knows I love her
But she's in love with him
I dream of one day taking his place
And every day and night I'll win

Being fair, he does deserve it
He spent years working day and night
It doesn't excuse the fact that I wish
I could beat him in a fight

There's no way we can trade places
I just want to live his life
I want the future he deserves
Now that his girlfriend is his wife

I'm his best man on his day
I must keep the monster hidden
I know these thoughts I have are stupid
I know they are forbidden

But I don't care, I'm jealous
Every time I see them kiss
I wish I was my so-called friend
My own life, no one will miss

The driving force behind many emotions and today's advertising, lust is a master of disguise. An animal instinct we all have and many take advantage of. Lust can be easily mistaken as a genuine sign of affection but it is nothing more than another act of selfish desire. When your emotions are all over the place they can be anchored back by the sheer power lust has all over us. It can drive anyone insane, and the means some people use to satisfy it leaves a very bitter after taste.

The Perfect Night
*

It's been a hard day in the city

My boss is on my back this week

I come home and the wife starts screaming

I missed an anniversary, but I don't care

I listen to her shout; she doesn't look attractive

She's not the young girl I fell in love with

I tell her I'm going out, but I don't tell her where

I've had enough, it's been such a bad day

But I know it will be a perfect night

I drive some miles away from home

A part of the city I know just about

There's a bar I've been to once before

A bar where the drinks are dirty and the women filthy

Parking my car around the corner, I step out

Pull my suit straight, turn my phone off

Entering the bar, I see two things

A seat free by the till, and a girl drinking to forget

I order my usual, but double it up
I send the girl next to me the same again
She looks like she needs it, and I know she likes it
She smiles at me, her lipstick looks fresh
And her eyes look as glazed as a regular drinker

As she looks to the bar, I shamelessly inspect her
Short-ish skirt, long slender legs
A smart shirt hugging every straight man's desire
I may have just eaten, but I'm already hungry

A few more drinks between us
She starts talking about why she's here
Something about her partner being stupid
I wasn't paying attention, trying to sound good
She's getting more and more interesting
I tell her lies about my life, pretending heart ache
She doesn't need to know my wife is alive
Or I'm struggling to make ends meet
At the end of the night, it's money well spent

Soon enough my plan starts to work
A hand on her knee, my tongue down her throat
The barman and drinkers look away in disgust
But soon we are out, I take her hand and we go

My car is only around the corner; I start being impatient

She doesn't know what she's doing, my perfect girl

Those strong drinks I got her are working for me

This is still going to be my perfect night

A short while later, she is out of my car

Her senses came quickly when she knew her mistake

But it doesn't matter, I got what I want

The memories from that are fresh in my head

As well as some buttons from her tight smart white shirt

I know I'm a beast but I'm too drunk to care

Taking advantage of a drunk desperate woman was a lot of fun

Even hearing her screaming brought a smile to my face

I sped away in the night, looking for girl number two

I'm going to make this, one hell of a night

Greed can be a very powerful and effective friend at times. It focuses purely on yourself, not leaving any room for anyone else. It is the difference between ambition and failure, but it is also the difference between friendship and loneliness. It doesn't matter what achievements you have thanks to greed, but it isn't a good thing to have on this road. It's a heavy burden but it is your choice to take it or leave it.

Quick Hands
*

Being greedy is easy, that's why I do it

It's only looking after yourself after all

But if you can profit from somebody else

You mine that gold vein leaving nothing but rocks

Count out your winnings, richly deserved

The quicker your hands, the more you can gather

Who cares if they need it more than you?

You want it, you grab it, that's the first rule

Your morals don't enter it, because it's only for losers

If your quick with your hands, you don't need your heart

You sit on your throne, you ignore all else

Your just glad that your quick hands have helped you again

Whenever it's something as small as stealing a phone

Or exploiting a company for as much as it's worth

Greed is my friend and greed is my life

It's hard not to feel the thrill of a steal

As long as you can rub it in people's faces

You pity those people who are honest hard workers

Being deaf to the anguish you leave behind
Works as well as being blind to what you cause
People know who you are and they're jealous
You may on occasion throw a bone
But a bone picked as clean as a whistle
If the hungry don't like it? Well stay hungry!

I'm too busy thinking about me
I could tell you I'm sorry but I'm not
The only time I want other people
Is when it's my turn to be exploited
Only then I demand that you help me
But don't expect anything in return

I'd do anything to make some quick money
I even risk a large sum here and then
On the racing, the ponies and dogs
All I can see are my potential winnings
If I win, then it's a genius idea
But if I lose I'm getting ripped off

My greed has taken over my life
If I lose everything I'll see that
Until then live life with your quick hands
But at the end of the day you realise
You can count your riches, your ill-gotten gains
But you cannot count people who care for you

Gluttony is a very quick and easy fix for anything negative going on. It's natural, people feel better when they are eating or have eaten and for some poor souls it's an emotion which they only have. It may feel good but it's hollow, worthless and dangerous. It's an emotion easy to be addicted to and just as hard to get out of. No matter what you eat or how much of it, it could never be the positivity you desperately need.

Uncomfortable Comfort

*

Being a kid was stressful
I found a way coping with life
The best thing in the world, eating

My parents would get into arguments
By shying away from breaking objects
I would run straight to the fridge

Bullies and teachers getting you down?
I would run to the nearest shadowy corner
And open my large size lunch box

I asked out a girl I liked earlier
When she laughed, I broke out my king size
Who needs to be kissed anyway?

I'm stressed about my exams
Why does my future depend on these?
Eating instead makes me calm

My skills are in cooking
I love working with food I enjoy
There are plenty of leftovers

My lifestyle causes me pain

My body's struggling to cope with food

But comfort is always important

So, what if I'm single

Shallow women are only interested in looks

Don't know what they're missing

I have a problem apparently

The problem is people don't get it

I'm struggling to cope obviously

It's my demon uncomfortable comfort

I'm terrified about eating to heal pain

But I start eating again

Always people point and laugh

They never bother to find out why

They only end up laughing

But food is my comfort

The one thing which never betrays me

It's my one true love

After years of constantly eating
It's a struggle for just going out
I've snookered myself right here

I'm the image of gluttony
There are people starving in the world
I've replaced emotion with food

When you start to feel pity, for yourself or for anyone, it is not the end of the road but it is a step in the right direction. Pity is a shallow form of selflessness and on the road to depression the impact it has on you is greater. You compare yourself to them and only then you realise you were being very selfish and stupid. There isn't too much of sadness in this world without you adding more.

I'm Not Them

*

Think of any ordinary person
But put them in a bad situation
A person who needs to meet challenges
But has been afraid of confrontation

Something which isn't their fault
But has seriously impacted their life
Something which can't be avoided
But has caused nothing but strife

Now just think on yourself
The problems which you do not have
But those poor people you've been thinking on
You have a life which they hungrily crave

Let's say you live in a flat
And you wish it was something more
Think of the people living on streets
Sleeping in bags on cold stone floors

Your job isn't all that you want
You dream of being able to get rid
Think of a poor unemployed mother
Who struggles daily to feed her kid

You have an argument with a loved one
You wish they would just go away
Try telling that to a child
Whose parents were taken that day

You wanted that brand-new TV
Your one is only four years' old
The old couple who can't pay for heating
Spending their winter in the cold

The countless millions out there
They have nothing at all to their name
Do you think of them when you splash out?
When you go to your local football game?

You think your childhood was rough
What of those poor children abused every day?
You weren't allowed out after dark
But their innocence was taken away

Your toe stubs as you miss the bus
You think your luck is on the slide
While next to you is a man in tears
On the brink of suicide

You sit in the warm, your able to eat
Your life isn't great like a gem
But you think of those people and it makes you think
I'm very lucky I'm not them.

It is shock which may have pushed you to be on this road, but it could be shock which may lead you to the way off it. Something which in an instant, changes the way you think. The way you see the world, the way you see yourself. You discover what you have become, what the consequences of your actions have caused and it leaves you speechless.

World's Collapsing

*

What have you become?

Start questioning yourself, what have you done?

This world has corrupted you, ask yourself how come?

Everything you built taken from underneath

Your falling fast but you're stuck in disbelief

Your emotions made you no better than a common thief

Your grief has done this to you

Falling through the air thinking what can you do?

Your world's collapsing all around you

These foundations you built around you

Gone, no longer there

You think your safe building them? Now your full of despair

If you think you can blame anyone, think again

It's your fault your feeling all this pain

All the people you pushed away

Al of the bad things you've done day after day

For everything you've done it's now time to pay

Your payment is your world tumbling down

Thinking you're a king, you've just lost your crown

What a fall from grace, your no king you're a clown

Are you shocked?

Well guess what, no one else is

We saw what was coming way before you did

We told you, but did you take our advice?

Any goodness you had locked away in a vice

You chose ignorance time to pay the price

What next now, what happens when you land?

Looking desperately around, looking for a helping hand?

But there's nothing, your sinking in quick sand

Your world's collapsing

Your life's relapsing

You want to rest but from now there's no relaxing

Be in shock the sun will never shine on your face

Buried underground, you have no time or space

Just think about that, think on everything you've read

All the emotions going on through your head

Everyone has it, this bitter moment called shock

You think your unique? Your just part of the flock

You want to speak out but you're afraid of being mocked?

No matter what is going through your mind

Don't be afraid of the help you want to find

Your whole world's collapsing

There's no avoiding it now

Look at your ruins surrounding you, no point asking how

You're the one to blame

Don't start thinking you have a claim

What's it all led to, this life of self-imposed fame?

You think you're the big dog? Your no better than anyone

Right here, right now, you're just a someone

Someone who's awake to who they really are

From being a good person, you've come very far

Doesn't matter what twisted you, who made you like this

Your dignity and pride, those things people miss

You chose to lose them for a bit more of bliss

What do you have when your whole world is gone?

You were winning at life, but you have not won

When you're lying there surrounded by the sins of your past

Thinking if there's a way you can fix this fast

It's a moment of shock, there's no need to panic

Though you've paid the price for being so manic

Realisation is the main turning point on your journey. You discover how much you have changed, what this depression has led to and the gruelling knowledge that you must finish this road the hardest way possible. There is no turning back from this point on, the path is open to you and you are now forced to see it through to its conclusion.

Sleeping Messaging

*

After a gruelling long day
You're in shock over who you've become
Your mind is exhausted

You climb into your bed
You wonder how you can possibly cope
Your tired eyes finally close

As you finally start sleeping
The nightmares start coming in full force
You know you deserve them

You see flashbacks and memories
The decisions you've made in your life
You wish you couldn't see

Every time you see them
A powerful voice calls over the nightmare
'These were all your choices.'

The people you love ignoring
The decisions you made which were selfish
Live with the choices tonight

The same strong voice calls
Telling you about what you did wrong
Your ears start bleeding furiously

This is only a dream
Why is it affecting you so much?
Your crying into your pillow

Your giving up on happiness
You think you can go no longer
You hear a new voice

It says you can change
Your doubting if you can trust it
You've had that disappointment before

The voice just calls louder
The nightmares start to lose their power
You haven't seen this before

You can change your life
All these nightmares they can go away
Pay attention to the voice

You wake up the next day
Not as upset as you were yesterday
Because today you have hope

The road ahead is long
You may think you cannot turn around
But remember the sleeping message

A major step is discovery. When our ancestors discovered new lands, they also discovered new opportunities, new ways of thinking and more importantly a reason to keep going. Even if it's changing the way you think about the world, it is none the less a major discovery. You have found a way off this road, you do not have to go down the dark path and no one else has shown you it, you discovered it for yourself.

A Different Way Home
*

Every morning and every evening you take the same way home

You drive down the motorway, past the same signs

You go off at the junction, that same old junction

Unconsciously turning left and right

The only changes you make are traffic related

The cold, grey only way home

Every day for years and years, the best years of your life

Driving the same route to the same job, the same life

You have been beaten down so hard your scared

Your scared of moving on, to see what's out there

You're a cog in a machine, a small cog

And driving the same road makes your small cog turn

You drive down the road which you've known for years

Not even knowing when you take the turns

The large supermarkets, the small boarded up shops

The homeless man you see on the park bench

The graffiti stained council estates where no futures lie

The greasy burger van parked outside your office

The next thousand hours pounding on your keyboard

Everything is grey from the walls to the eyes

The sun sinks as low as your spirits as you leave

Another journey home you will never tell in years to come

Time to go home little cog, rest up for the next day

Just make sure you don't take any detours

You are forced to take a detour home

Some poor soul decided he couldn't be a cog

So, you cannot take the motorway home

For the first time, you are forced to take a left

Left at the closed down family butchers

Your forced to keep your eyes open, for directions back home

However, you start to notice many other things on the way

The sun shines differently in this town

The sun shines on different windows in different windows

The people here have different looks on their faces

There isn't a boarded window anywhere you can see

And there isn't any single grey shade in sight

Surprisingly you start to crack a smile

Your eyes are more open than they have been in years

You don't just look left and right when you need to turn

You turn left and right like you're on top of a mountain

And below you as far as your eyes can see is the world

A world where the sun is beaming down, a world full of beauty

A world you can explore, touch, experience and brave

Far different to the world your used to

This is the world you forgot, the world you chose to leave

Many people are forced to leave, but few can return

For a small moment in your dull grey world

Your eyes are not closed, you are alive and free.

This is the one emotion you need to take that scary first step on that long road to recovery. Courage will be your companion, guide and helping hand all in one. When you go those first few steps courage will lead you through it. It burns in you, burning from a desire to get through all these obstacles depression has put in front of you. It knows it's starting to lose and will try everything to get you back but not while you have courage.

Message in The Fire

*

A fire has the power to kill

But it's not its only purpose

It's not just destructive power

Which lies on its surface

A fire can protect as well as harm

It's an anchor in the sea of night

When the shadows outnumber and surround you

Your backed up by the flames burning bright

A power which protected us all

As we left blinking from those old caves

To now burning bright in old oil drums

The setting of loud modern raves

What do you feel when you look into the fire?

You feel warmth, you can feel the power

But the fire has a message for you

Listen to it in this darkest hour

The fire has courage if you see through the danger
The fire can open your eyes
The fire can conquer the fear in your soul
The fire can quell all your cries

The history of man is filled with these stories
Of brave men and women with fire
They burn in their souls and they overcome all
Even when everything seems dire

The moment its darkest before the dawn
Courage is needed by all
So, let that fire burn in your heart
Until you hear the cockerels call

Here is the message which you need to read
The one which relates to you most
Do not be scared to be who you are
Don't cower behind image and boast

Let your fire burn as you like
Please don't let it burn out
Your fire is what keeps you going
It's courage you can't live without

This world today has such ice
The absence of fire is strong
Don't put your fire out and give up
It isn't the world where you belong

Listen to the message in the fire
The greatest message you can receive
The fire takes you out of the nightmare
The fire will make you believe

At long last, you start to feel something great. You get back your sense of wonder, a stage where your eyes are open fully for the first time since you set off. You are not looking at yourself, you are looking around at what you have missed but which you can go back to. You start to notice brand new surroundings which your clouded mind has hidden from you and you are drinking it all in the energy of a child's very own sense of wonder.

My Mausoleum, My Lighthouse
*

Going away to some distant lands

From the tallest mountains to the desert sands

Seeing the greatest structures built from human hands

Standing proud above us for centuries and

Time cannot forget such wonders there are

Whether you go around the corner or travelling far

If the world is a sky, it's the brightest star

So far but when you arrive and look for yourself

Your raking in all this cultural wealth

And you smile so much it's good for your soul

It's taken so long but your finally whole

It's so intense you cannot help but ponder

Your life is so trivial compared to this wonder

Why are you focusing so much on today?

Just focus on these wonders which make you want to stay

There are so many worldwide you cannot run out

It's like you don't have a reason to pout

The Pyramid of Egypt, so strong and so tall

Christ the Redeemer watching over us all

Even the wonders we cannot see now

Fallen beauty so historic it survives somehow

These wonders live on as the time and age changes

From height, beauty, natural, they cover such ranges

This world is so ugly; it can make you curl up

The person it makes you makes your spirit breakup

There is beauty still out there

You just need to know where

Discover these wonders they are all around

These majestic structures so tall and so proud

Some look so great they appear so loud

Others have subtle beauty which needs to be found

The Seven Wonders, six may not have survived

But each one so memorable they cannot have died

The great marble tomb, the height of devotion

To the lighthouse, man-made guardian of the ocean

From the temple, which says can rival the Gods

To the desert gardens which have defied the odds

A statue and colossus which although they are gone

Like the others, through history, they always live on

Escape from the city, built from rough concrete blocks

Look out at the ocean breaking on all those rocks

You don't have to go far to look at these wonders

A moment in the park is better than plunder

For some a wonder isn't just what you see

A wonder is a thought, an idea, a way to feel free

Go find your wonders, don't take it from me

You can stay at home and quiver like a mouse

Or go out, discover your Mausoleum or your Lighthouse.

There is no better feeling in the world than on the day you finally get your optimism back. From now on the depression cannot get at you, it is trapped way back on that road but there are still a few steps to take. However, with your courage and your sense of wonder back, you know you can finish it. Optimism is a beautiful thing to regain during the end stages of depression because it keeps you on the path and no chance of getting off.

New Day, New Dawn

*

The darkness will end soon

The sun is only on the horizon

A new dawn always comes

No matter what's out there

The darkness can hide many evil things

That's why people fear it

The darkness fears the dawn

The light makes it turn and run

Do not run with it

Stand and face the light

It is better than staying in shadows

Nothing can hide in light

The sun's warmth is cleansing

Open your arms and let it in

Wear it like a coat

A new dawn for everybody

It's never too late for your own

It is never too late

People are scared to change
They find it easy in the dark
There's no risks to take

The darkness is very bittersweet
Not only can it hide the fear
It can hide almost anything

The dawn can hide nothing
The dawn brings everything into the open
The dawn sees through you

Please step into the light
There's no need to hide much longer
The night is almost over

The glass is half full
There is an end to the nightmare
A new day is ahead

You should start smiling inside
You need to take this second chance
Or the darkness is yours

Don't listen to anyone else

Just do what is best for you

You should trust only yourself

The night has finally gone

Stand tall in this brand-new dawn

No need to be afraid

When joy returns, it is like walking from the deepest, darkest cave and being bathed in warm sunlight. Pure joy is the final purging of darkness from your mind and refills your poor empty heart, but more importantly it is the end of the road you started. You have survived and come out of the depression as a stronger person, and if that isn't a joyous occasion I don't know what is.

Toothless Smiles
*

You have escaped the dark and the nightmares
You have a chance to rebuild your life
For the first time in years you can smile again
A smile as bright as your first ever smile
A smile filled with joy and innocence
A toothless smile

The old you is stuck in the past
There's a new you waiting out there
The only help you need is your own
You don't need anyone to tell you how to smile
It's your own smile, your unique smile
A toothless smile

The world is filled to the brim with colour
There is so much light and air it's breath-taking
The smiles you have are seen by all
The smiles you give are on other people's faces
Because you can smile after what you've been through
These toothless smiles

The ones you love are loving you more

The cold distant you is just that, distant

You can hear it calling you back but keep going

The grass is greener on the other side

The feel of this brings a smile to your heart

The toothless smiles

People find it easy to forgive you you're past

You have turned your life around

You're no longer sulking in the dark

The world is ready for the new you

Let everything go and just smile

A toothless smile

Let the joy of living fill your soul

Life is no longer a burden but a blessing

You were not born just to pay bills and die

You were born for this beating heart, for this beautiful world

The world is more beautiful now your smiling again

Your toothless smile

You find joy and wonder in everything
Every step a skip in your heartbeat
Fall in love every day until you die
But you die with a smile on your face
You have lived life as it was meant to be seen
Those toothless smiles

Why are these smiles so toothless?
The first time your smile is born
At a time when your soul is so pure
So, go back to the smile you were born with
The most innocent smile in the world
A toothless smile.

Confidence is something you have lost on the road, feeling it fall from you like a warm jumper on a frosty day. But when it comes back to you, it is like the return of an old friend, or the return of a lost dog. You were lost without it but now it is back and you have no fear of ever going back. You now have the confidence you need to deal with your life, you cannot see the future but you are ready for whatever it throws at you.

Broken Mirror
*

You see a mirror in your path

This mirror judges you like a sociopath

It tells you what you want to hear

It preys upon irrational fear

You see your reflection, crystal clear

So, clear it mocks you

It rocks you

Shakes you till you cry out in pain

Leaves you in tears, it's brought the storm you bring the rain

The cyclone which blows your mind

You stare at this mirror; you see what you find

You look like a clown; you call yourself ugly

You listen to those people who shout it out with glee

It's a gypsy's curse, you ask why always me

This mirror shows you a monstrosity

You give up

You've surrendered this fight

There's no reason you should see the end of this night

To live in a perfect world, you have no right

The only thing to do is gain some height

From a chair, with a handful of rope

Your tired of not being able to cope

There isn't even a glimmer of hope

So nope, your done in this world, tie the knot

Make a noose, get hooked up, make the chair hot

Move your feet, it will be over soon

It won't be too long to escape this gloom

Just look at the mirror, at the loser you see

Just rock your feet and count to three

One ...

Two ...

...

Wait

What's that in the surface?

A crack? Get off that chair and start looking in earnest

This perfect thing which has harshly judged

It's not completely flawless, its broken and smudged

You take down that rope, get off the damn chair

You start seeing that your life is fair

This reflection you hate is no better than you

You think about the torture it's put you through

Calling to your now imaginary hates

Makes decisions for you, calling out your fates

You think back to some memorable dates

Where insecurity kept you locked at the gates

So many chances you lost, all because of this

A light come on in your head, you're getting the gist

You take that hangman's rope, wrap it round your fist

It's time you lived your life so now take charge

Think so little of yourself time to think large

Look at the rope, it nearly got severe

You smile at last as you put your fist through the mirror

Look at that, what the mirror was hiding

You've been living in gloom, here comes a flash of lightning

Stop hiding in the mirror room go out into the world

Let everyone see you, all your flags unfurled

Step into the light, the whole world is watching

So, give them a show because no one is judging

With the mirror gone there's no stopping you now

The world is yours my friend, so stand up, take a bow.

The meaning of life is to be happy. If you are not happy you have nothing to live for, no reason to carry on. It is losing happiness amongst others which is the reason you were on that road in the first place. It is an important emotion, one which everyone needs and one which can make the world change for the better.

Priceless

*

There are many things you can buy which make you happy

But being happy itself is completely priceless

Nothing in this life is free

But the best thing in life is being free

Your happiness is your bread and butter

It's your perfect ten, your hundred percent

They say bad things happen to good people

But you're a good person who can change that

Have no doubts, all doubts have a price

But being happy is priceless

Become happy for the smallest things

And the smallest things will make you happy

Do not wait on an impossible dream

They can break the biggest hearts

Your dreams should be to become happy

A dream which cannot be broken at all

You can become happy any time of any day

Anyone can come to you tomorrow and make you happy

Cut the costs as you cut out depression

Because being happy is priceless

Think of a funny joke when your sad

Or a treasured memory when you cannot cope

They do not cost money, nor should you need to use it

Any sort of happiness is priceless

Many people think pride is a bad thing to boast about, after all it is one of the seven deadly sins, but pride after depression is the complete opposite. You have spent so much time thinking only negative thoughts about yourself, a burst of pride at what you have achieved is proof that what you have been through has made you a stronger person than before.

Sweat, Dirt, Tears and Pride

*

The farmer plants his seeds

Working day and night in deep summer

The farmer has his pride

Every day he sweats away

The same jobs for all his life

His tears are pure pride

No one can upset him

He takes pride in what he does

Sweat, dirt, tears and pride

The farmer's mind is healthy

The farmer has the right to happiness

His happiness is in pride

He is a proud man

People should be more like the farmer

His years of hard work

All achievements deserve some pride

It doesn't matter how big they are

You should always feel proud

The farmer can see his
Now you should feel your own pride
Be proud of yourself

Everyone has their own pride
They find it their own unique way
But they always find it

You should go find yours
No one can show you your pride
It's something only you know

Be proud of being yourself
Frame it for the world to see
You should only impress yourself

Pride is always hard fought
A battle that should always be fought
The winner's reward is pride

When the day has ended
What makes you smile as you sleep?
Knowing you've regained your pride

It's something you cannot see

But everyone can see it in you

It's your badge of honour

Stand on you own feet

What have you lost, but also gained?

Sweat, dirt, tears and pride.

The True Value
*

What is the meaning of life?
A question everyone will ask
People spend all their lives looking
But fail in this impossible task

I can't say that I have the answer
But what I think it is may stun you all
It isn't the collection or wealth
Or waiting for your life to un-stall

My answer is the true value
It's what everyone is seeking
The feeling of falling in love
Which you get from a first meeting

When your eyes are first together
When you're both too shocked to speak
You reccive a dazzling smile
Which strikes like an eagle's beak

You don't want them in your bed
You want something different
You want to be in their lives
You want to be significant

A voice you can hear forever
Even screaming down your ear
You want them in your life
Every day, every month and every year

The way you feel holding hands
And simply looking in their eyes
You can see whole galaxies
And endless starry skies

Keep that love in these modern days
When every pair of lover's cries
You feel a love which last forever
Because real love never dies

There could be days which your far apart
On different sides of this spinning world
Hold each other together in your hearts
And your two destinies are together twirled

Love isn't perfect like in the movies
There is no music when you are together
You never know at the end of a film
If the couple stay with each other forever

There are good days but there are always bad
Arguments, disagreements and spite
However, that is nothing when your love
Is worth conceding every other fight

My meaning of life is to love
Don't be scared to show how you feel
Love is the one true valuable thing
Because true love is undoubtedly real.

Thank you so much for reading my book
The story behind it is real
I haven't just written it to cash in
Or get some kind of big deal

Do not follow my mistakes
Don't keep insecurities bottled up
Or you will forever be searching for answers
At the bottom of a glass beer cup

Depression will always be hard
But follow the trail of these words
There will be good times in the future
Positive emotions will flock to you like birds

This book takes you through the range
From loneliness, which once I couldn't cope
But I put these feelings on paper
Now turn the page and discover hope.

*

The Scarecrows
*

The sad and lonely scarecrow

Still guarding over the field

Staying guard every day, putting off the dancing crows

For countless days and endless nights

Always alone, always sad

The farmer looks one day at the sad and lonely scarecrow

He decides there and then he should fix the problem

The farmer walked up to the scarecrow and started work

He spent an hour making it perfect

The scarecrow couldn't see and he had no idea

Hours later the sad and lonely scarecrow swayed in the wind

He swung and what he saw changed his world

An old frayed dress, a tattered straw bonnet

Two long poles and a waiting smile

A second scarecrow

That night as the witching hour struck

The magic of the scarecrows bloomed

They left those long poles, hand in hand

They set off through the fields

To start their new lives, together forever

Printed in Great Britain
by Amazon